Google Certified Professional Cloud DevOps Engineer

Exam Cram Notes

First Edition

Chapter 01: Introduction

Certification Exam Overview

Professional Cloud DevOps Engineer Certification Overview defines a role, not a certification or an exam because Google's Certifications are tied to a job task analysis.

A Professional Cloud DevOps Engineer ensures that development processes are efficient and that service dependability and delivery pace are balanced. They know how to design software delivery pipelines, deploy and monitor services, and manage and learn from incidents using Google Cloud.

The Professional Cloud DevOps Engineer exam measures your ability to do the following:

- Apply the ideas of site reliability engineering to service.
- Improve the efficiency of your service.
- Implement strategies for service monitoring.
- Construct and deploy CI/CD pipelines for a service.
- Manage service issues.

This exam validates that you are the person the job role has described. To do that, you have to go through a 2-hour exam after paying an exam fee of $200. Instead, you will have to understand a question and select the correct answer from multiple options for the question. There are multiple-choice or numerous select questions.

You can give an exam online or at a local test center. In either case, you would not have access to tools or any other reference material. There are no pre-requisites required for this certification exam. Still, since it is not an entry-level exam, Google recommends you to have 3+ years of industry experience and 1+ years of experience managing solutions on GCP.

Exam Guide Walkthrough- DevOps Engineer Job Role Description

A Professional Cloud DevOps Engineer ensures that development processes are efficient and that service

reliability and delivery pace are balanced. They know how to create software delivery pipelines, deploy and monitor services, and manage and learn from incidents using Google Cloud.

The term **"Professional"** in the definition implies that this role exists in the context of business. **"Cloud"** means that the company is taking advantage of cloud technology such as GCP. The word **"Engineer"** clearly states that the principles and practices of engineering are core to the rule. We should accurately engineer solutions.

Another side of the term "develop the system" is "run the system" — that is, millions of people using the software can rely on your software.

"Balance" is the center of the entire role since the DevOps role requires things to be perfectly balanced.

"Service" could be a single component or an entire web server API. Here, it could be a whole application or a database. We call it service because it does something, and it should continue doing it.

"Reliability" says all about it should continue doing it. What good is a system which is not available when you need it? Also, what good is a system which is available but still does not do what you need to do. Operations are essential, but the development side is also vital.

"Know how to design software delivery pipelines using GCP," says all the previous software development skills in the Google Cloud Platform. **Design software delivery pipelines** is a crucial thing for SRE or DevOps engineers. Computers are very robust and accurate compared to humans, so we should program a computer to go through all of the software details for us. We should also program computers to monitor for us. They should stay vigilant.

Chapter 02: Foundation and Concepts

Introduction

This chapter focuses on delivering applications in GCP with a DevOps focus. DevOps on Google Cloud can help you save time and money when developing software. Understanding how these services work is essential for improving the efficiency of your software development processes.

Google Cloud Fundamentals

This chapter also covers the fundamentals of working with Google Cloud Platform, including vocabulary and concepts (GCP). Many of the Google Cloud Platform computing and storage services, such as Google App Engine, Google Compute Engine, Google Kubernetes Engine, Google Cloud Storage, Google Cloud SQL, and BigQuery, are discussed and compared. You will learn about the Google Cloud Resource Manager hierarchy and Google Cloud Identity and Access Administration, and other critical resource and policy management tools. Hands-on labs teach you the fundamentals of working with GCP.

What is (the Business of) Software Development?

Software Development

Every aspect of our lives is influenced by software. Today, all industries benefit from software development, whether in sales, marketing, or customer service. Whether you are searching for new music, ordering groceries, creating an email campaign for your business, or setting your home alarm system from your phone, you are using the software. Many processes that were once burdensome and time-consuming are now automated by enterprise software. And its presence in our daily lives and businesses is only going to grow.

What is a Software Development Company?

Depending on the organization, a software development company (or team) creates custom software applications, frameworks, and tools to aid in problem-solving or achieving a specific goal. This team members are, as one might expect, extremely intelligent. While each software development team or company is different, they will typically include software architects or developers, at least one product owner (the person responsible for testing and working with the product to ensure it functions properly), and some sort of project manager.

What is a Software Development Company's Process?

While developing custom software tools and applications is as difficult as you might think, the process is quite simple. While each software development team will spin things, customers will go through a process similar to the one below.

Identify the Problem or Need

A good company will take the time to fully comprehend your issue, budget, goals, and desired outcome. To ensure that this partnership is a win-win for all parties, both parties should clearly understand what success entails.

During this time, your software development team should get a sense of what kind of software will best meet your requirements. For example, will an app, an intranet, or a website (such as Hubspot or SalesForce) best serve you?

Create and Develop

After working closely with you, the software development company will begin developing your custom software to get this project off the ground. They will start with a visual wireframe to help you "see" what your product will look like, and then they will begin coding it. You do not want to pay for rushed custom

software, just as no one wants to live in a house built in a day. Make sure you understand what to expect in terms of communication to stay up to date on progress and when you will be able to request edits.

Test and Troubleshoot

It must be tested and used once your software has been developed. Before your tool goes live, your software development team will thoroughly test it to ensure it functions properly and achieves your objectives. The team's product owner will use the software in the same way that your ideal customer would, noting any issues that may arise: glitches, slow loading speeds, random shutdowns, and so on.

Distribute

When your product is finished, the software team will help you distribute it through the appropriate channels, such as the App Store, email, or social campaigns.

Importance of Software Development for Your Business

Once your product is complete, the software team will assist you in distributing it through the appropriate channels, such as the App Store, email, or social campaigns.

Improves sales and service

Software development propels your company to new heights of incorporation. It aids in promoting and spreading your business by making your brand visible to everyone and almost anywhere via a computer or smartphone.

Promote your business

Understanding what your customers think of your brand and products is critical. You must have an online platform that allows customers to easily reach out to you and share their thoughts on your products and services if you want to know their opinion and have them leave a positive comment.

Direct communication

The only thing that can help you communicate directly with your clients is software development. No other strategy can help you communicate directly with your customers. It is the most efficient method of increasing brand awareness.

Increases customers' engagement

Every company wishes to expand its customer base. But how can a company increase its customer base? The solution is online marketing. Businesses must implement online marketing strategies. You can increase customer engagement with the help of a mobile app or website, causing them to return to you rather than your competitor.

Helps in marketing your business

Software development enables you to use on-the-go marketing for your business, allowing you to promote your products and services at any time and from any location without spending any extra money or time. From any part of the world, customers can contact you.

Benefits of Google Cloud Dataflow

Like many other Google Cloud Platform capabilities, dataflow is meant to make running your business easier in the digital transformation era. The system can even collaborate with third-party developers and partners to make data processing chores more efficient. It works with Salesforce, Cloudera, and ClearStory, for example. The following are some of the advantages of the Google Cloud Dataflow system:

The capacity to simplify organization operations: The GCP's serverless strategy reduces the operational overhead of cloud performance while delivering significant security, availability, scalability, and compliance. You can also troubleshoot and monitor pipelines while they run using Stackdriver, allowing you to respond quickly to any issues that arise.

Friendly pricing: The Cloud Dataflow model charges you per minute for jobs based on how much you use the available resources. This means you don't have to pay for something you are not using right now.

Accelerated Development: Cloud Dataflow offers easy, rapid, and effective pipeline construction strategies with the Apache Beam SDK, which provides a rich set of session and windowing analytics, as well as an ecosystem of the sink and source connection solutions.

A starting point for machine learning: Including the TensorFlow Cloud Machine Learning APIs, you can leverage your Cloud Dataflow strategy as an integrating

point for your AI solutions with real-time personalization cases.

Operations

The responsibilities of teams throughout the software lifecycle will undoubtedly evolve as firms reorganize for DevOps. Throughout the software lifecycle, operations teams that have traditionally measured themselves on uptime and stability—often operating in silos apart from business and development teams—become collaborators with new stakeholders. Teams from development and operations begin to collaborate closely to construct and improve their delivery and management methods.

What is a DevOps Engineer?

A DevOps engineer implements processes, tools, and methodologies to balance needs across the software development life cycle, from coding to deployment to maintenance and updates.

A DevOps Engineer is familiar with the Software Development Lifecycle and various automation tools for developing digital pipelines (CI/CD pipelines).

DevOps Engineers work with developers and IT personnel to oversee code releases. They are either developers who are interested in deployment and network operations or sysadmins interested in scripting and coding and move into development to improve test and deployment planning.

What does a DevOps Engineer do?

A DevOps Engineer understands the Software Development Lifecycle and numerous automation techniques for creating digital pipelines (CI/CD pipelines).

DevOps Engineers work with developers and IT personnel to oversee code releases. They are either developers who get interested in deployment and network operations or sysadmins who become interested in scripting and coding and transition into Development to better test and deploy plans.

A DevOps engineer must understand the IT infrastructure that supports software code in dedicated, multi-tenant, or hybrid cloud environments. They may be required to allocate resources, select an appropriate

deployment model, direct testing protocols to validate each release, and monitor performance after release. Preparing test data, analyzing results, troubleshooting issues, and communicating to software developers are possible tasks.

What is a Site Reliability Engineer?

SRE is defined as "what happens when a software engineer is asked to build an operations function." Developers would hand over their code to IT specialists in the traditional architecture of segmented IT operations and software development teams. IT would then be in charge of system implementation, maintenance, and any on-call responsibilities associated with the system in Operation. Fortunately, DevOps arrived and forced engineers to share in-production systems, own their code, and take on-call duties.

SRE and DevOps are two current operations methods that were born out of a need to address issues such as:

- Our production environments and development processes are becoming increasingly complex.
- Rising business reliance on those ecosystems' continued operation
- The workforce's inability to scale linearly with the size of these situations
- The requirement to move more quickly while maintaining operational stability

Both operational techniques place a premium on topics such as monitoring/observability, automation, documentation, and collaborative software development tools, all of which are critical in dealing with these difficulties.

Between SRE and DevOps, there is a lot of overlap in terms of tooling and areas of work. "SRE believes in the same things as DevOps, but for slightly different reasons," according to The Site Reliability Workbook.

Developing a Google SRE Culture

In many IT businesses, the motivations of developers, who seek agility, and operators, who strive for stability, are not matched. Google uses Site Reliability Engineering (SRE) to match incentives between development and operations and provide mission-critical production support. Adoption of SRE cultural and technical approaches can aid in improving business-IT

collaboration. This course covers Google SRE's key practices as well as the critical role that IT and business leaders play in SRE's organizational adoption success.

Primary Target Audience

IT and business leaders who want to embrace the SRE paradigm. CTO, IT director/manager, and engineering VP/director/manager are just a few examples of roles.

Secondary Audience

This content may be beneficial as an introduction to SRE for other product and IT jobs such as operations managers or engineers, software engineers, service managers, or product managers.

Benefits of SRE

SRE resources and tools to help your operations and SRE teams perform more smoothly

SRE principles can be used to track the health of a service

Using built-in service monitoring support, keep track of the health of your services and collaborate with developers to boost change velocity. To reduce risk in your service, choose metrics for SLIs, create SLOs, and manage error budgets. To reduce MTTR and swiftly answer queries regarding service health, use powerful dashboards to collect data and logs, including golden signals.

Increase automation and reduce toil with out-of-the-box integrations

To swiftly troubleshoot situations, use our built-in interfaces with the tools you already use. Safely implement progressive rollouts and rollbacks. As part of your CI/CD, you may use pre-built Cloud Build connectors to build, test, and deploy artifacts to Google Kubernetes Engine, App Engine, Cloud Functions, Firebase, and Cloud Run.

For quicker resolution, combine all views into one

Get a unified view of all logs, events, metrics, and SLOs in one place. Get in-context observability data from Google Kubernetes Engine, Cloud Run, Compute Engine, Anthos, and other run times' service consoles. With no setup required, collect metrics, traces, and logs. You can do real-time log management and analysis at scale thanks to sub-second ingestion latency and a terabyte per second ingestion rate.

Get extra assistance from Google Cloud SRE experts

If you require more hands-on assistance during your journey, we offer additional services such as Google consulting.

Drive collaboration between SREs and developers to achieve "shift-left" observability

Developers can instrument and export trace data to Cloud Trace using OpenTelemetry (OT) tools and Google Exporter. Our new unified Ops agent (currently in preview) collects metrics and logs and supports OpenTelemetry for capturing and transporting measurements. Many of our cloud offerings are being updated to include OT libraries as standard capabilities. One example of this work is Cloud SQL Insights.

Chapter 03: Balancing Change, Velocity, and Service Reliability with SRE

Introduction

Before the era of DevOps teams, there were two teams. One was the development team, whose focus was on new features and getting them to market as quickly as possible. On the other hand, we had an operations team whose focus was on keeping everything running smoothly, while the updates by development teams often disrupted the ops. These were two different teams with different rules, objectives, and priorities. So, to cope with this problem term, DevOps came out. This term was developed by Andrew Shaffer and Patrick Debois around 2008.

DevOps Infinity Loop

The infinity loop starts with planning, and after that, we move into the creation phase, where the development team will verify creation. Once they verify it, they package it and release it into the market. From there, it enters a world of operations where the app is configured to run as smoothly as possible. Smooth operations require constant monitoring. When it is running smoothly, we can plan for the next project.

Key Pillars of DevOps

- Reduce organization silos: the idea is to remove the environment where teams compete against each other for different objectives and bridge teams together for common objectives. To do this, we need to increase communication, leading to a shared company vision.
- Accept failure as normal: in a DevOps world, too many failures are not only normal but a success. You try to anticipate, but failures are bound to occur. It is foolish to think an app is secure, especially the growing one. Failure helps learn, and when you have such a culture, people are more forthcoming about their actual responses and actions.

- Implement gradual change: gradual change opens the door for continuous change. Small updates are better than large upheavals, which can cause operation failure. Small changes make it easier to review the app, and they are easy to reverse.
- Leverage tooling and automation: automation reduces manual tasks and frees up time for other tasks. Tooling and automation are the heart of CI/CD pipelines that make up so much of DevOps. It speeds up the work and adds a layer of consistency, which is very important, especially when troubleshooting is concerned.
- Measure everything: measurements are key; they tell you when things are going right. Automation tools like CI/CD need constant monitoring, and DevOps need synthetic and proactive monitoring.

Site Reliability Engineering (SRE)

SRE is a concept defined by google engineer Ben Traynor in 2003, who stressed reliability. Here are some key points raised by Ben in a talk in 2014:

1. Does the product work? No matter how many features a product has, what good it is if it does not work?
2. He defined reliability as an absence of errors.
3. Unstable services likely indicate a lot of issues. Therefore, people must attend to reliability all the time, not only when there is a real emergency.

SRE=DevOps (The Google Way)

This formula is very famous by DevOps that is its class SRE implements DevOps. Or, you can say that DevOps is what and SRE is the *how*. Now we can see the pillars of DevOps in terms of SRE since there are so many parallels.

SRE looks at the reduced organization silos as sharing ownership. The developers and operations teams are involved in a project from the start and not separately. They need to share the same tools and techniques to make it easy to share ownership of the project.

To accept failure as a normal of DevOps, SRE says no-fault post mortems and SLOs. It implies that no one is blamed after an incident is resolved, and when the incident occurs, an SLO (our service-level objective) was not properly met. The key point is never to repeat the same failures and to track incidents using Service-level incidents (SLIs). SREs, ensure that there are not too many failures even if they teach us something. This formula for balancing incidents includes mapping SLIs with objectives or SLOs.

To implement a gradual change of DevOps, SRE suggests reducing the costs of failures. They do this by limiting canary rollouts by first testing small portions of users and then expanding the user base. This affects fewer users, where they want to keep automation where possible for cost reduction.

Leverage tooling and automation are pretty much the same, as both SREs view automation as a force multiplier. They want to use autonomous automation, which centralizes mistakes and makes it easier to respond.

Pillar SRE uses measure toil and reliability to measure everything, which is key to SLOs and SLAs. SREs want to reduce toil and up engineering time. It is important to monitor constantly to reach an accurate level of what service level is.

Service Level Indicators (SLIs)

SRE is broken down into three different functions. First, we define availability which maps to Service Level Objective. Then we determine the level of availability which maps to Service Level Indicator. Then we indicate what happens when this availability fails and is mapped to Service Level Agreement. In this lesson, we will see how the level of availability is determined.

What is SLI?

SLI is a measure of quantifiable reliability, or in other words, SLI can be a carefully quantitative measure of some aspect of the level of service. SLIs are metrics over time specific to the user journey, such as request/response time or anything that shows how well a service is doing. Some of the examples of SLIs are:

- Request Latency: How long it takes to return to respond to a request
- Failure Rate: A fraction of all rates received: (unsuccessful request/all requests)
- Batch Throughput: proportion of time = data processing rate > a threshold

User Journey

A user journey is a sequence of tasks that are central to user experience and crucial to service. For example, an online website user journey may include product search, adding products to the cart, and checking out after shopping.

Consider a request/response journey. Some of the SLIs according to this journey can be:

- **Availability:** Proportion of valid requests served successfully
- **Latency:** Proportion of valid requests served faster
- **Quality:** Proportion of valid requests served to maintain quality

None of the SLIs are directly connected to the user journey: searching for a product, buying it, and ending purchase are all part of it.

The set of SLIs for the data processing user journey will be different. It could be:

- **Freshness:** Proportion of valid data updated more recently than a threshold
- **Correctness:** Proportion of valid data producing correct output
- **Throughput:** Proportion of time where data processing rate is faster than a threshold

The list is non-exhaustive; it may include a proportion of valid data processed successfully.

Google's 4 Golden Signals

Google has identified 4 such SLIs that it calls the Golden Signals. It includes:

- Latency or the time it takes to fulfill the request

- Errors or the rate at which service fails
- Traffic or how much demand is directed at your service
- Saturation or a measure of how close to fully utilized service's resources are

Transparent SLIs

Google's developed transparent SLIs help you monitor Google Cloud Services and their effect on your workload. It will also tell you about whether google cloud services are behaving normally. Here is a dashboard for APIs and services. There are three charts, one for traffic, the other for errors, and the third for latency. If you find a correlation between your app's degraded performance and sustained increased latency, you might want to call Google for help.

SLI Best Practices

- Limit the number of SLIs because too many SLIs can lead to contradictions and produce difficulty for operators
- Reduce complexity because not all metrics are good SLIs and can generate false positives
- Prioritize the journey by selecting the most valuable user and identifying user-centric events
- Collect data over time and calculate a rate, average, or percentile
- Not all requests are the same. Requesters may be human or bots. Thus, combine requests for better SLIs
- Collect data near to user at the load balancer

Service Level Objectives (SLOs)

In this lesson, we will review how SLOs define the level of your availability. One hundred percent of reliability is not a good objective. Because 100% reliability is very complex and expensive, take your reliability where users do not realize the difference. Moreover, the resources you use for ensuring 100% reliability can be used for developing and launching new features.

How SLOs are Tied to SLIs

SLOs are directly related to your SLIs; SLIs measure SLOs. These measurements can be single values or ranges of values, such as most commonly SLI <= SLO, or if you are working with ranges (lower bound <= SLI <= upper bound) = SLO. If you are working with percentiles, some

of the common percentiles are 99.5%, 99.9%, or 99.99%. They are often referred to differently, such as 99.99% as 4 9s or 99.9% as 3 9s.

Another way to relate SLOs with SLIs is that SLIs are metrics that detail the health of a service, for example, site homepage latency request < 300ms over last 5 minutes @ 95% percentile. SLOs are agreed upon bounds for how often SLIs must be met. For example, 95% percentile homepage will succeed 99.9% over next year.

Service Level Agreements (SLAs)

In this lesson, we will explain what happens if the availability is not maintained with SLAs. SLAs concisely say: should reliability fail, there will be consequences.

Characteristics of SLAs

- SLAs are like formal documents. This is a business-level agreement SRE is not involved in drafting SLAs, except for setting SLIs and their corresponding SLOs
- The contract can be explicit or implicit. In implicit, SLA terms are not explicitly spelled out. For example, Google does not have a contract with millions of users, but its unavailability can cause serious damage to its revenues
- Explicit contracts contain consequences, such as a refund for paid services or service cost reduction on a sliding scale
- These days SLAs are offered on a per-service basis

How SLAs Relate to SLOs and SLIs

SLIs drive SLOs and SLOs inform SLAs. Suppose your SLOs are at 200ms, and we want to set our SLA at a higher value. Suppose at 300ms, and beyond that, we have got into a serious problem. So, your SLAs must be achievable; SLOs set the internal targets that guide prioritization. It represents the desired user experience and tells us missing objectives should also have consequences. SLAs set the level of service just high enough to keep customers from jumping ship. SLA incentivizes a minimum level of service, and you want to give some space between SLO and SLA, so your ongoing reliability targets your SLO, and you easily meet your SLA.

Chapter 04: Generating SRE Metrics

Introduction
This chapter will help you learn about the Site Reliability Engineer (SRE) metrics, monitoring reliability, and monitoring data. It also discusses metrics, text logging, structured event recording, distributed tracing, and even introspection.

Monitoring Reliability
Monitoring allows you to gain visibility into a system. It is a core requirement for judging service health and diagnosing your service when things go wrong.

Monitoring can be defined as "collecting, processing, aggregating, and displaying real-time quantitative data about a system, such as query counts and types, error counts and types, processing times, and server lifetimes."

Benefits of Monitoring
- *Analyzing long-term trends:* Monitoring will give you the perspective of looking at your operations over time, which is critical for setting SLOs.
- *Comparing over time groups*: You cannot view only one-time series, but you can, of course, compare values over multiple periods.
- *Alerting:* Monitoring is the best way to provide real-time alerts, which is critical to keep your cloud computing operation up and running smoothly. The key here is real-time.
- *Exposing in dashboards:* You can visualize your operations right on the screen in various dashboards, so you can monitor those dashboards if need be and get the information you need as things happen.
- *Debugging:* Monitoring also enhances ad hoc retrospective analysis, or in other words, it has terrific debugging capabilities.

- *Raw input for business analytics:* While business analytics is not strictly an SRE responsibility, providing those insights will help those whose responsibility it is.
- *Security breaches analysis:* Monitoring can also be a big help when trying to track down security breaches.

Types of Monitoring
The two types of monitoring are as follows:

Black Box Monitoring:
Black box monitoring is the monitoring of servers, emphasizing things like disc space, CPU utilization, RAM consumption, load averages, and so on. These are the basic system metrics that most industry would consider important to monitor.

White Box Monitoring
The monitoring of apps running on a server is known as White box monitoring. This can range from the number of HTTP requests received by your webserver to the response codes issued by your application.

Monitor Resources:
Metrics
Metrics are numerical measurements that represent the attributes and events of your service. The primary tool that works with metrics on the Google Cloud Platform is Cloud Monitoring, which used to be called Stackdriver Monitoring. This is truly universal, as it collects a huge amount of metrics from all the services at Google. These metrics are not as detailed as logs, but they are almost immediate, very close to real-time, and better for alerts.

Logging
A log is a record of events where the events are appended or added one after the other. The Google service that takes care of this is called Cloud Logging, which used to be called Stackdriver Logging. Logs are

very detailed and contain huge amounts of highly granular data, so much so that it is often difficult to sift through the log until you find what you are looking for. Now, because this is so granular, the processes involved mean that it is not as real-time as metrics, and there will be a delay between when the event occurs and when you can see it in the logs. However, you can run logs through a batch system and then query them with a system like BigQuery, and you can also visualize them onto dashboards,

Use case:

- One of the best use cases for logs is digging into problems, really trying to find the root cause of an issue, which is often more easily identified in a log than in a metric.
- Another excellent use is creating detailed reports using the log's processing systems.

Alerts Principle

Alerts can be defined as "Alerts give timely awareness to problems in your cloud application so that you can resolve the problems quickly."

How Alerting Works?

1. Setup Monitoring

First, you will need to set up your Google-powered eagle eyes, and we want to do that by setting up a series of conditions that are always being monitored. You will find that this is critical, especially for SREs, to keep track of their SLOs.

There are two different types of conditions that you can work with. The first can look for a missing metric over a specified time. It indicates that some pipeline operation has failed, or you can also look for a threshold to be exceeded, like the desired SLO.

2. Track Metrics over Time

The next step after setting up the monitoring is to track those metrics over time. Time is vital for SLOs because an alert might often be fired if the tracking reveals that a certain condition like high latency persists over five minutes. You cannot set a time window for a long period, such as a week, as the maximum is 24 hours.

3. Notify When Condition Passed

The third step is to notify whoever is selected when a condition is met, using whatever system you have in place. When that happens, an incident is created and displayed in your monitoring system. Alerts can be sent through various means, including email, SMS text message, various apps like Slack, or even Cloud Pub/Sub.

But, how do you know when to set up an alert? Well, a key factor is how fast you are burning your error budget, and there is a formula that you can apply to find out.

Burn Rate:

Startups and investors use the burn rate to track the monthly cash that a firm spends before generating its income. The burn rate is also used to calculate its runway or the amount of time before it runs out of money.

Types of Burn Rate Policies.

There are two different types of burn rate policies:

1. Slow Burn Alerting Policy:

The purpose of this type of burn policy is to let you know that your error budget is in trouble before the end of the compliance period. Slow burn alerting policies are not as urgent as the fast burn conditions because the increments in consumption can be relatively small and need a comparatively long lookback period. The term lookback period means that it determines how far back in time you are retrieving data. Critically, it is also used as the compliance period for calculating the SLO performance and the error budget. So, the threshold to watch should be just above your baseline because you are looking at a longer period where even tiny amounts of increase could add up.

2. Fast Burn Alerting Policy:

The fast burn policy is a bit more urgent than the slow burn alerting policy. Because these are such intense changes, the lookback period can be much shorter than with a slow burn policy. Unlike slow burns, the threshold can be much higher than the baseline, like 10 times higher. So, a fast burn policy looks for a big unexpected change in consumption that could burn off your error budget for an entire quarter in just a couple of days. And

if you set it too low, that is going to result in multiple false positives.

Establishing An SLO Alerting Policy

1. Select SLO To Monitor:

First, we are going to need to choose the SLO that we are monitoring. It is generally best to monitor just one SLO for each alerting policy

2. Construct a Condition for Alerting Policy:

We want to build out those conditions for the alerting policy. You will likely have multiple conditions, one for the slow burn and another for the fast burn.

3. Identify the Notification Channel:

Multiple notification channels are available: email, text, pager, apps such as Slack, general webhooks, and even the Google Cloud Service Pub/Sub.

4. Provide Documentation:

Providing documentation is an optional but highly recommended step that includes the information your team will need to resolve the alert's problem. You can do this as part of the entire policy to deliver it whenever the alert is sounded.

5. Create Alerting Policy:

You want to bundle all these pieces together to complete your alerting policy. You can do this either directly in the console or using the Google Cloud API.

Investigating SRE Tools

SRE Tools
SRE-developed tools are typically created by and for systems engineers to solve the challenge at hand. SREs rarely create tooling for a company's external clients, sales representatives, or product managers.

Development Tools
These are the services you will use when building your CI/CD pipelines as part of the development process.

Google Kubernetes Services
Google pioneered Kubernetes to run containerized applications; containerized apps can scale up and down with ease and make global computing feasible. This service shows that pedigree Kubernetes runs on Docker images.

Container Registry Services
The container registry service's sole purpose is to place Docker images. This makes the continuous part of CI/CD not only possible so that images can be easily updated and deployed but also straightforward.

Cloud Build
It automates the process and follows your designated series of steps to quickly and easily create, test, and update your apps and then push them live in a controlled manner. A big part of living the CI/CD is making sure that you can continuously develop, and these next two services make that possible.

Cloud Source Repositories
Cloud Source Repositories provide a home for completely Git-compatible reports that can be updated as needed and integrate seamlessly with Cloud Build and the Container Registry.

Spinnaker for Google Cloud
Spinnaker for Google Cloud gives you the power to trigger pipelines when Cloud Build finishes its job, as well as extend additional Cloud Build stages to your pipeline as needed.

Operations Tools
Operational tools services rely on:

Cloud Monitoring
It is critical to track metrics, provide visualizations on a dashboard, and send alerts for all your cloud-based apps.

Cloud Logging
It offers granular detail and append-only format on every operation of every service on the Google Cloud Platform.

Services For Making Your Operation Run Reliably, Smoothly, and More Efficiently

Cloud Debugger
Cloud Debugger is an essential service when the system encounters inevitable issues. You can do this in real-time without impeding its output.

Cloud Trace
Cloud Trace maps trace out exactly how your service is processing the various requests and responses it

receives, all while tracking valuable latency details and presenting them for analysis.

Cloud Profiler:

Just as Cloud Trace watches requests, Cloud Profiler keeps an eye on your code's performance, looking for bottlenecks as the code executes in production so you can increase efficiency and reduce costs.

Chapter 05: Understanding Google Cloud CI/CD Pipeline

CI/CD on Google Cloud

Continuous Integration and Deployment (CI/CD) pipelines ensure that your functions work locally as well as in a Google Cloud test environment.

You can use a CI/CD platform like Cloud Build to run your existing Cloud Functions tests on a regular basis once you have finished development locally. Continuous testing ensures that your code is still working as it should and that your dependencies are up to date. Because Cloud Functions are not automatically updated, you can use CI/CD pipelines (including those built on Cloud Build) to test and redeploy your functions from a source repository like GitHub, Bitbucket, or Cloud Source Repositories.

Continuous Integration

At its foundation, Continuous Integration (CI) is about obtaining feedback early and often, which allows you to spot and fix problems early in the development process. Instead of waiting for a massive integration later, you integrate your work regularly, often many times a day, with CI. Each integration is tested using an automated build, allowing you to identify and resolve integration issues as rapidly as possible.

Continuous Delivery

Continuous Delivery (CD) is an extension of Continuous Integration (CI). The purpose of a CD is to package and prepare software in order to distribute incremental modifications to users. Release risk can be reduced and release confidence increased using deployment tactics such as red/black and canary deployments. The use of a CD makes the releasing procedure safer, less risky, faster, and, when done correctly, boring. Developers can focus on building code rather than changing deployment scripts after CD has made deployments painless.

CI/CD Benefits

According to Martin Fowler, an American software developer, the following are the benefits of the CI/CD system:

- The CI/CD system breaks barriers between customers and development by distributing a new piece of code to users rapidly
- The code is distributed rapidly and then used, and you can get fast feedback on those updates. This means that you can be more collaborative in the development cycle
- It is dramatically easy to find bugs in a new system using a CI/CD system. This leads to dramatically fewer bugs in the system
- CI/CD system also reduces the risk of failure

Relating SRE to CI/CD

In this lesson, we tie SRE to CI/CD. You do not need to implement CI/CD because you are asked to do so but understand why this makes sense. The purpose of SRE is to make better software faster, and CI/CD is one of the tools to accomplish it. Continuous Integration is a software development process in which team members integrate their work regularly, usually at least once per day, resulting in several integrations. To detect integration faults as quickly as possible, each integration is evaluated by an automated build (including tests). Many teams have discovered that taking this strategy reduces integration issues and produces more coherent products faster.

SRE Principles

The Google book on SRE book lists the principles that underline SRE, many of which tie to CI/CD. We have talked about embracing risk and eliminating toil by reducing manual work.

Continuous Integration

Continuous Integration is a software development process in which team members integrate their work regularly, usually at least once per day, resulting in several integrations. To detect integration faults as quickly as possible, each integration is evaluated by an automated build (including tests). Many teams have discovered that taking this strategy reduces integration issues and produces more coherent products faster. The context is people are working on a big project, and when they are making changes, their changes are usually independent of another person or team. So instead of integration after a lot of work has been done, it is better to do it a little bit at a time.

Purpose of Continuous Integration

The act of just binding the changes into one code base is not enough. The core idea that happens is that each of these integrations gets automatically built and tested, leading to the purpose of continuous integration, ensuring that the updated codebase is at least functioning and is not completely broken. This is a quality bar. Continuous integration goes a bit beyond just being able to compile it.

GCP Continuous Integration Concepts

Challenges faced by large organizations when they work with large software development teams are when multiple developers are working on the same code base or related systems. Some of these challenges are listed below:

- It is difficult to coordinate updates between multiple developers on a complex system
- If developers work on interrelated portions of software, this can lead to incompatible updates, leading to bugs and errors in the software
- Organizations that do not follow rapid-release DevOps mindset applications are released frequently and with large updates, resulting in many bugs to fix at a time

What is Continuous Integration?

At its foundation, Continuous Integration (CI) is about obtaining feedback early and often, which allows you to spot and fix problems early in the development process. Instead of waiting for a massive integration later, you integrate your work regularly, often many times a day, with CI. Each integration is tested using an automated build, allowing you to identify and resolve integration issues as rapidly as possible.

Within minutes, you can generate automated builds, run tests, provision environments, and scan artifacts for security vulnerabilities using GCP's continuous integration capabilities.

CI has numerous benefits, like the smaller changes you keep integrating result in fewer bugs to troubleshoot. The faster changes result in rapid feedback loops, which helps us to resolve issues quickly. Such benefits result in a better return on investment.

The overall CI process has five components:

- Source: There is a shared source repository
- Build: From the source code, you can build your new code
- Test: Test your code
- Report: Once you build and test code, you want rapid feedback or report that your building or testing was successful
- Release: If the testing is unsuccessful, fix bugs; otherwise, release software to the new operation

Continuous Delivery

Continuous Delivery is a software development methodology in which software is built so that it may be deployed to production at any time. Many organizations have not yet started with the CI/CD process, so releasing the product at any time is quite scary to them.

Purpose of Continuous Delivery

The purpose of Continuous Delivery in the CI/CD pipeline is to ensure that the updated codebase is at least as good as it used to be, so it is releasable. The delivery here means that the update is as good as it can be delivered to businesses, and they can deploy it whenever they require. They do not have to deploy it, but they can whenever they want. This is also a quality bar.

Regression

Regression testing evaluates a software product's behavior after it or something it integrates with has changed. However, there are several types of regression

testing, which many businesses overlook. Checking original code after a new integration or analyzing how a tiny update affects performance during peak workflow are examples of regression testing. Patches are also subjected to regression testing before being released to verify that they do not add flaws. Another popular form of regression testing is determining how the software performs after any upgrades were made to allow for operation on a new operating system. To protect against risks, all of these must become part of DevOps' process.

Continuous Deployment

Automatic deployment aids in the speeding up and reduction of mistakes in the process. It is also a low-cost solution because it employs the same tools you deploy into test environments. Automatic deployment emphasizes if you have a deployable build, you deploy it.

If you are used to a process that is an error-prone system, then doing that automatically does not reduce errors. Continuous Deployment is low-cost because it uses the same system as that of the Continuous Delivery system.

Automated rollback is an additional automated tool to consider if you deploy to production. Sometimes bad things happen, and it is nice to be able to swiftly return to the last known good condition if nasty brown particles touch revolving metal. The ability to automatically revert relieves a lot of the stress associated with deployment, enabling people to deploy more frequently and get new features out to consumers faster, which is the reason we want people to be comfortable with continuous deploys.

Purpose of Continuous Deployment

The purpose of continuous deployment is to make the newly updated and validated codebase available to the users. Continuous deployment is not a quality bar but the automation of an action. The quality of the bar was set in the Continuous Delivery stage. Continuous deployment requires excellent automated testing in that continuous delivery stage. Now that the newly updated codebase is

available to users does not imply that this new functionality is available to the users.

The risk of making any change is larger when the known impact of that change is larger; you should try to reduce the impact of change instead. Your metrics should show that the change has no visible impact on your users.

Feature Toggles

Feature Toggles (also known as Feature Flags) is a powerful approach that allows teams to change system behavior without changing the code. So, if you can modify the system without modifying code, you can also modify code without modifying behavior. When you add changes to a system to make something new, you continuously integrate new changes into a system. To stop those unfinished changes from breaking the entire system, you should put your changed functionality behind a feature flag to protect the default behavior from changes.

Your feature flag is off until you are ready to let users use it, and in this way, you can manage the rollout of the feature independently from the rollout of changed code. Your half-finished feature might be deployed several times, but since its impact is managed with a feature flag, it would not have been causing problems. When you fully roll out a new feature and are sure that you do not want to roll it back, you can remove your feature flag to simplify your codebase.

GCP Continuous Deployment Concepts

There are multiple steps in the software delivery process, starting with raw source code and a deployed application running in production for your customers. Starting with source code in the source code repository, building and testing code, storing code in artifact management and deploying build code into production. In other words, we have raw source code, then we build the container, store the container, and then deploy that container.

Chapter 06: Cloud Source Repositories

Introduction
This chapter will learn the transition from our initial overview of continuous integration concepts by now focusing on the first step in the CI process, specifically focusing on Google's native repository option called Cloud Source Repositories.

Cloud Source Repositories
Cloud Source Repositories transmit repository activity logs to Cloud Logging by default. It can be used to track and troubleshoot data access. You can use these logs to assess current repository synchronization, other users' repository access, and administrative activity like creating removals and permission changes.

Characteristics Of Cloud Source Repositories
- You can create, develop, and manage your code in a secure manner
- You may effortlessly collaborate on a fully featured, scalable, and private Git repository
- Connecting to other Google Cloud technologies will allow you to extend your Git price

Cloud Source Repositories Key Facts:
- *Fully Managed Private Git Repository:* **You can** build, test, deploy, and debug code right away
- *Native GCP integration:* **It helps in** integrating cloud build, cloud functions, cloud operations(formerly stack driver), and more
- *Sync/mirror third-party repository:* One-way mirror from GitHub/Bitbuckets to CSR(Cloud Source Repositories)

Features Of Cloud Source Repositories:
- *Source Browser*

  Using Source Browser, you can see repository files within Cloud Source Repositories. Focus your view on a specific branch, tag, or commit by applying a filter.

- *Perform Git Operations*

  You can set up a repository as a Git remote. You can also push, pull, clone, log, and do any other Git activities workflow requires.

- *Automatic Syncing*

  Connect Cloud Source Repositories to a GitHub or Bitbucket-hosted repository. When updates are pushed to GitHub or Bitbucket, automatically sync them to Cloud Source Repositories.

- *Proven Reliability*

  Manage your code on globally spread systems across several data centers and run on Google's high-availability infrastructure.

Chapter 07: Artifact Management with Container Registry

Introduction

In this chapter, we will discuss the next link in the full CI/CD process. The chapter will discuss concepts related to artifacts management and focus specifically on Googles' Container Registry Service.

Container Registry and Artifact Registry

Introduction

Initially, the container registry was the primary location to store and manage your different container images, including Docker containers. However, in spring 2020, Google announced a new service called Artifact Registry, which would act as the eventual successor to the Container Registry Service.

Artifact Registry

Artifact Registry, the evolution of Container Registry, is a centralized location for your business to manage container images and language packages (such as Maven and npm). This makes it simple to link it with your CI/CD tooling to create automated workflows.

Container Registry:

Container Registry is a centralized location for your team to manage Docker images, conduct vulnerability assessments, and select who has access to what using fine-grained access control. Existing CI/CD connectors enable you to create completely automated Docker pipelines for quick feedback.

Difference between Artifact Registry And Container Registry:

The main difference between container registries and Artifact Registry is that the container registry can only manage containers. Artifact Registry will have the same purpose, and then it can also store and manage containers. However, it will also be able to store and manage other artifacts such as Java packages, node.JS packages, Tarballs, binaries, and much more. Think of it as a much more expanded version of the Container Registry Service that we have today.

Aircraft Management

Artifact management acts as the bridge between the end of the continuous integration process and the beginning of the continuous delivery and deployment process of the CI/CD cycle from a high-level perspective. Once again, our continuous integration process starts with raw source code hosted in some shared repository, such as Cloud Source Repositories, and third-party services such as GitHub and Bitbucket. From that source code, our various continuous integration tools such as Cloud Build and third-party tools such as Jenkins and Travis CI/CD automatically take that raw code and then do some sort of automated packaging and testing process on it. After these continuous integration tools complete their building and testing process, they need to push or store that package code into some storage container for deployment into our services. This storage and management location is referred to as artifact management.

Benefits of Artifact

Working with artifacts can be difficult because they come from various sources inside and outside an organization. Each system with which you interact provides a potential point of failure owing to outages or other problems. A single build may contain files originating from:

- Several internal teams carry out builds
- GitHub hosts open-source projects
- Sites dedicated to certain formats, such as Maven Central and Docker Hub

An artifact management solution addresses these complexity and reliability challenges by centralizing your artifacts in a single location. You have more say over your artifacts and how they are used. An artifact repository:

- Serves as your artifacts' single source of truth and CI/CD integration point
- Version management, vulnerability scanning, and approval workflows are among the capabilities available
- Allows for centralized access control and consistent setup
- Consistency in your automation for working with artifacts is provided
- Many DevOps skills are supported for optimizing organizational performance
- Version management, vulnerability scanning, and approval workflows are among the capabilities available
- Allows for centralized access control and consistent setup
- Consistency in your automation for working with artifacts is provided
- Many DevOps skills are supported for optimizing organizational performance

Concepts of Container Registry

Container Registry is a private Google cloud-native container image registry, which can currently support both Docker and OCI image formats. A common theme that you may notice so far with other Google cloud-native CI/CD tools is that it has native integration with other Google cloud services by default. One interesting and important fact that you need to be aware of is that you do not store images in the Container Registry Service when working with Container Registry; rather, when you are pushing and pulling images into and out of Container Registry, those images sit in a cloud storage bucket. Container Registry, by comparison, is merely the management layer for managing those container images in that cloud storage bucket, and Container Registry is also a key part of a DevOps mindset.

Characteristics of Container Registry

Secure, Private Docker Registry

Using container registry, you will have access to secure private Docker image storage on the Google Cloud Platform within minutes. The container registry controls who can see, download, or access photographs and get

continuous uptime on an infrastructure that Google secures.

Build and deploy automatically

When you commit code to Cloud Source Repositories, GitHub, or Bitbucket, images are automatically built and pushed to a private registry. Create CI/CD pipelines with Cloud Build integration or deploy directly to Google Kubernetes Engine, App Engine, Cloud Functions, or Firebase.

In-depth Vulnerability Scanning

Container registry enables you to identify vulnerabilities early in the software deployment cycle. Check to see if your container images are safe to deploy. A constantly maintained database ensures that your vulnerability scans are always updated with new malware.

Lockdown Risky Images

Container registry uses native integration with Binary Authorization to define policies and prevent image deployment that violates the set policies. It automatically locks down container images to prevent potentially dangerous images from deploying to Google Kubernetes Engine.

Native Docker Support

Container registries create numerous registries based on your need. Push and pull Docker images to your private Container Registry using the normal Docker command-line interface. Docker may be used while searching for pictures by name and tags.

Fast, High-availability Access

You can get the fastest response time globally by utilizing GCP's regional private repositories located around the world, storing photos near your computing instances in Europe, Asia, or the United States, and using Google's high-performance worldwide network for quick deployment.

Access Control

Container Registry uses cloud storage rules to determine if you have permission to either push an image or pull an image into and out of Container Registry. Access control is the number one priority if you push images into Container Registry or edit images already inside that require either the storage admin role or higher. Suppose you merely need to read images or pull images out of

Container Registry into some other service. In that case, you will need, at a minimum, the storage object viewer or a higher-level role as well service account interactions with the Container Registry Service, which in actuality is the cloud storage service.

Artifact Registry: the next generation of Container Registry

In order to manage their software supply chain, enterprise application teams must manage more than containers. That is why we built Artifact Registry, a fully managed service that can handle both container images and non-container artifacts.

Artifact Registry enhances and expands on Container Registry's existing features, such as customer-managed encryption keys, VPC-SC support, Pub/Sub alerts, and more, laying the groundwork for huge security, scalability, and control improvements. While Container Registry is still available as a Google Enterprise API and will continue to be serviced, new features will only be available in Artifact Registry in the future, and Container Registry will only get major security fixes.

Container, OS, and language repositories all have a common control plane.

You can store multiple artifacts in the Artifact Registry, including OS packages for Debian and RPM and language packages for popular languages like Python, Java, and Node. As a developer, you can store multiple artifact formats, including OS packages for Debian and RPM and language packages for popular languages like Python, Java, and Node. You can also control them all from a single, unified interface.

Cloud IAM provides a more granular permission model.

Cloud IAM provides fine-grained access control for Artifact Registry. Unlike Container Registry, this allows you to manage access to individual repositories rather than the entire project's images. This allows you to target rights as precisely as possible, such as to certain regions or contexts.

Repositories in your preferred region

Artifact Registry lets you create regional repositories, which allows you to store your artifacts and data in the exact spot where they will be utilized, resulting in increased availability and speed. You can only use "multi-regions" in Container Registry; for example, the closest multi-region for Australia is Asia. You can, however, create a repository directly in the Sydney datacenter with Artifact Registry's regional support.

A pricing approach that takes your location into account

While Artifact Registry's cost is still determined by a combination of network egress and storage usage, regional repositories allow you to pick where your container repositories are hosted. Although Artifact Registry's per-unit storage prices are greater, optimizing the locations of your repositories to be hosted in the same region where they are utilized can save money because network traffic within the same region is not considered egress and so is free.

A vital component of a safe supply chain

Artifact Registry was built from the ground up to work with our secure supply chain solutions. This means it can scan your container images for vulnerabilities as they are submitted to Artifact Registry, and it can work directly with Binary Authorization to safeguard your deployments.

Chapter 08: Spinnaker

Spinnaker Concepts

In this chapter, you will learn about the spinnaker software product role in CI/CD pipeline. All CD tools are very complex. We are focusing on Spinnaker versus other CD tools like Jenkins. If you go through the documentation on DevOps, there is an underlying theme that they favor Spinnaker as a cloud-native CD tool. Spinnaker was co-developed by Google in conjunction with Netflix.

What is Spinnaker

Google and Netflix collaborated on Spinnaker, an open-source multi-cloud continuous delivery technology. In a recent blog post, Google announced the Spinnaker for Google Cloud Platform, allowing clients to install and run Spinnaker on the Google Cloud Platform (GCP).

Spinnaker for GCP makes setting up a production-ready configuration on the Google Cloud Platform a breeze. It interacts with Google-managed runtimes like Google Kubernetes Engine (GKE), Google Compute Engine (GCE), and Google App Engine (GAE), making it simple for teams to build, test, and deploy to those services. It also interfaces with other Google services such as Cloud Build, Binary Authorization, and Stackdriver, allowing clients to expand their CI/CD pipeline while also incorporating monitoring, compliance, and security.

Customers can benefit from Spinnaker's production-ready configuration in the following ways:

Secure Installation

Cloud Identity Aware Proxy (IAP) supports one-click HTTPS configuration, giving you control over who may access your Spinnaker installation.

Automatic backups - a Spinnaker installation's configuration is automatically and securely backed up for auditing and fast recovery.

Integrated auditing and monitoring

As previously indicated, spinnaker connects with Stackdriver, which simplifies the monitoring, troubleshooting, and auditing of modifications and deployments.

Simplified Maintenance

Configuring Spinnaker to deploy to new GKE clusters and GCE or GAE in other GCP projects are just a few of the aids available to simplify and automate the management of Spinnaker installations.

How Spinnaker Works

Most of the deployments of the pipeline are done via KubeCTL commands and manipulating different YAML files. Spinnaker creates YAML files and will apply those YAML files via KubeCTL commands. You are still creating deployments, updating your replica sets with different versions of your application or different versions of your containers, creating load balancers with services. The only difference is Spinnaker is automatically running KubeCTL commands and creating and managing YAML files behind those commands.

There are different ways of implementing Spinnaker. Consider a method where we install Spinnaker deployment directly onto GKE, and then it will handle the deployment to the same cluster it is installed on. We start with a shared code repository from which we will use CI products, such as Cloud Build, to build, test, and package our code into a container. Then push that container into artifact management, in this case, represented by Container Registry. Finally, we deploy containers on Kubernetes Engine, which in this case will be automatically handled by Spinnaker.

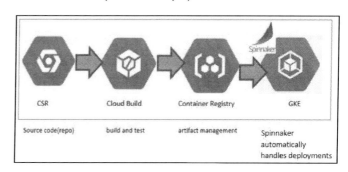

In this whole process, we have to perform only two steps manually. First, we have to commit our code to the repository. Secondly, we have to approve a cut-over from the staging environment to our production environment at the end of the process.

Chapter 09: Full Development Pipeline

Introduction

This chapter will put CI/CD concepts together for a fully automated end-to-end CI/CD demonstration using a custom application.

Full CI/CD Concepts

Teams can use Continuous Integration (CI) and Continuous Delivery (CD) to automate software construction, testing, and deployment. It will then walk you through the CI/CD pipeline stage, showing you how to use Container Registry and Cloud Build to build and deploy an application to GKE.

In this chapter, we will look at:

- End-to-end CI/CD pipeline
- Full CI/CD demonstration
- Setting up our Spinnaker environment
- Using the Google-provided good hub in guided Cloud Shell demonstration
- Create the rest of our application pipeline
- Deploy in manage our custom application within our pipeline
- Perform optimization on our Docker images so that they are slimmer and are less vulnerable

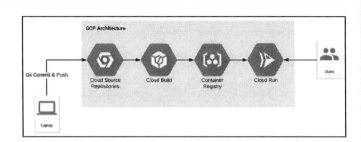

We will start with a Cloud Source Repository, which will contain the code for our unique world gift art application and copy it from our GitHub repository. Then, we will establish a Cloud Build trigger on any commit to our Cloud Source Repository. Cloud Build will take our code, package it into a Docker container, and push it to the container registry automatically.

Cloud Build will also submit our Kubernetes YAML files to Spinnaker, managing those Kubernetes files on our behalf. Cloud Build will also publish messages to a pub/sub and notify when additional containers are available to handle. Once our containers have been posted to a container registry and Spinnaker has been notified of new pictures, Spinnaker will take those images, run them through a staging pipeline to check for issues, and then manually approve them to push them out of our production pipeline. Our bespoke application, designated world gift art on the far right, will have its persistent backend in a cloud storage bucket and a structured database in a cloud data store.

Chapter 10: Troubleshooting OCI Services

Introduction

This chapter will cover the service's core features and why they are so significant, particularly from an Operations/SRE standpoint. Then, we will look at how Cloud Trace monitors an application's latency. We will go over several examples of Cloud Trace's capabilities that are accessible via both the Google Cloud dashboard and the Cloud Shell. We will discuss how API access is crucial to Cloud Trace, and we will look at Cloud Profiler, regardless of whether your app is running on a compute engine VM, Kubernetes engine cluster, or one of the app engine environments. We will also run some code and look at how Profiler can show you how much CPU and memory is consumed by the various functions involved.

Introduction to Optimize Performance with Trace/Profiler

Google App Engine applications are now automatically instrumented by Cloud Trace. It continually examines all App Engine requests and analyses each endpoint-level trace regularly to uncover performance bottlenecks and insights.

Currently, Cloud Trace analyses billions of traces per day and generates millions of reports. It regularly inspects your application requests for various factors, such as Memcache size, datastore batch size, cursor usage, and other data, looking for ways to improve your application's efficiency.

For example, when the offset is large, utilizing a cursor to make datastore queries may be more efficient than using an offset. When Cloud Trace detects a call pattern with an offset that causes the program to slow down, it displays an insight with a recommendation to use cursors. We constantly enhance existing insights and introduce new insights to Cloud Trace to give accurate and effective ideas.

What the Services Do and Why They Matter?

Cloud Monitoring and Cloud Logging are specialist services that focus on specific areas of your apps' ongoing activities.

Cloud Trace

A distributed tracing system that collects and shows latency statistics from your applications via the Google Cloud Console is known as Cloud Trace.

Operational Management

Operations management (OM) is the administration of business procedures inside an organization to achieve the best level of efficiency achievable. It is concerned with transforming materials and labor as efficiently as feasible into goods and services to maximize profit. The following are some Operational Management concepts.

Debugging

Inspect the condition of your application in production at any code point without halting or slowing down requests.

Performance Management

It offers continuous profiling of resource consumption in your production applications alongwith cost management.

Latency Management

Provides latency sampling and reporting for App engine, including latency distributions per-URL statistics.

Security Management

With Audit logs, you have near real-time user activity visibility across all your applications on Google Cloud.

Google 4 Golden Signals

Implementing Google's four golden signals is an eccentric place to start when developing a monitoring solution. Latency, traffic, errors, and saturation are the gold signals.

Latency

The time it takes to send a request and receive a response is a latency. Latency is generally assessed from

the server-side, but it can also be measured from the client-side to account for network speed disparities. Your operations team has the most influence over server-side latency, but the client-side delay is more important to your customers. It is also critical to understand when stressors in your application's environment affect or do not affect your end-users.

The target threshold you select will depend on the type of application. A human on a mobile phone may demand a substantially faster response time than an automated system, such as an API or ad server. You should also track the latency of successful and failed requests separately because failed requests frequently fail quickly without any additional processing.

Traffic

The quantity of requests traveling over the network is traffic, and examples are HTTP queries to your web server or API or messages sent to a processing queue. Peak traffic periods can put additional strain on your infrastructure and push it to its limits, causing downstream repercussions. It is an important indicator because it distinguishes capacity issues from poor system setups, which can cause problems even when there is little traffic. It can also help you design capacity for distributed systems to meet expected demand ahead of time.

Errors

Errors might alert you to infrastructure misconfigurations, problems in your application code, or faulty dependencies. A surge in error rate, for example, could signal a database malfunction or a network outage. It could imply issues in the code that survived testing or only surfaced in your production environment after a code deployment. The error message will provide you with more information about the specific problem. Errors can also impact other measures by artificially decreasing latency or causing frequent retries, which can saturate other distributed systems.

Saturation

The load on your network and server resources is defined by saturation. Every resource has a capacity beyond which performance degrades or becomes unavailable. It includes CPU use, memory usage, disc capacity, and operations per second. Understanding your distributed

system design and experience is required to determine which service areas may become saturated first. These data are frequently leading indicators, allowing you to alter capacity before performance deteriorates.

Cloud Trace Primary Features

The following are the features of the cloud trace:

Easy setup

After a brief configuration, all Cloud Run, Cloud Functions, and App Engine standard applications are automatically traced, and libraries are available to trace applications running elsewhere like VMs, App Engine, and containers (GKE, Cloud Run).

Performance insights

Each endpoint level trace is automatically assessed for performance bottlenecks.

Automatic analysis

For each traced program, daily performance reports are generated automatically. Moreover, reports can also be generated on demand.

Extensibility for custom workloads

To track applications running on virtual machines and containers, the Trace API and language-specific SDKs are provided. The Trace API can ingest trace data via the Cloud Trace UI.

Latency shift detection

Your application's performance data are examined over time to identify the latency degradation of your application.

Cloud Profiler

Cloud Profiler defines as constantly monitoring the performance of CPU or memory-intensive tasks running across an application. With support for Java, Go, Node. Js, Python, and Cloud Profiler enable developers to examine applications operating anywhere, including Google Cloud, other cloud platforms, or on-premises.

Cloud Profiler Primary Features

Cloud Profiler is a low-cost statistical profiler that continuously collects CPU use and memory allocation data from your production apps. The following are the features of the cloud Profiler:

- Reduce Cost

- Improve Performance
- Save Profile for 30 days
- Export Profiles for longer storage
- Agent-based
- Extremely low-impact
- Support Java,Node.js, Python, and so on

Instrument Your Code For Cloud Trace

Your application must be instrumented to send traces to Cloud Trace, and the Google client libraries can be used to instrument your code. However, it is advised that you instrument your application with OpenTelemetry or OpenCensus. These are tracing packages that are open source, and the chosen package is OpenTelemetry, which is actively being developed.

Client Libraries

Google is migrating to using OpenTelemetry libraries across all languages. It is a collection of open-source tracing and statistics instrumentation libraries that work with various backends, and you can keep using the OpenCensus libraries.

Three Steps to Setting up Cloud Provider Outside GCP

1. Enable Profiler API inside Google Cloud Project by enabling stack driver Profiler API after creating a project.
2. Get credentials for the Profiling agent; there are two ways to do this:
   - Use a service account with private-key authentication
   - Use Application Default Credentials (ADC)
3. Configure the agent by passing in the project ID via a **config()** or similar method.

Chapter 11: Identifying Application Errors with Debug/Error Reporting

Service Introduction

When things go wrong, the first step in fixing them is to be aware of the problem. This lesson is devoted to understanding how GCP error reporting works and how you can make most of its services to identify and fix an issue quickly.

Troubleshooting with Cloud Debugger

With a cloud debugger, you can inspect code in real-time without stopping or slowing it down. You do not have to add a bunch of print statements outputting variables in the call stack and test your system to death before deploying a fix and seeing if that works. Moreover, with Cloud Debugger, you can work with code from multiple resources, and you can quickly find code in a specific file, function, method, or line number. Cloud Debugger allows you to work collaboratively to share your debug sessions by sending a URL.

Key Workflows

The two important Cloud Debugger tools are Snapshot and Log Points. A Cloud Debugger snapshot captures the application state at a specific line location. In a snapshot, you can grab local variables and the entire stack. You can take snaps conditionally in Java, Python, and Go. Snapshots support canarying, so you can quickly check them as you roll out your new versions.

Log Points allow you to inject logs into running apps without redeployment. These log points remain active for 24 hours if you have not deleted them or redeployed the service. Log Points also support canarying, and you can add Log points conditionally. The output is sent to the target's most appropriate environment.

Establishing Error Reporting for your App

Google Cloud Error Reporting can notify you when a problem has occurred and been noted in the logs. Error reporting is available in a wide range of applications: PHP, Java, Python, .NET, Node.js, Go, and Ruby.

Error Reporting Notifications

Error reporting notifications are automatic, but you have to enable them for each project. The person being notified must have the proper role or permissions set up. They must have Project Owner, Project Editor, Project Viewer role, or Custom role with cloud notifications like activities.list permission. The people with these roles will automatically receive an email. You cannot customize the email, but you can forward the email to an alias or Slack channel. If they have a mobile app, there will also be an error.

Correcting Code with Cloud Debugger

Cloud Debugger is a Google Cloud Platform tool that allows you to check the condition of an application at any code point without having to halt or slow it down. Cloud Debugger makes it easy to see the current status of an application without having to add logging lines. Cloud Debugger works with all versions of your software, including test, development, and production.

Chapter 12: Monitoring, Managing, and Maximizing Google Cloud Operations

Service Introduction

Learn how to track, debug, and enhance the performance of your infrastructure and applications. This chapter will teach you how to monitor the entire stack, manage and analyze real-time logs, debug code in production, and profile CPU and memory utilization.

Monitoring, managing, and maximizing Google Cloud operations is a must-have knowledge that is meaningful to the DevOps engineer. In this chapter, we will focus on operations in the context of Google Cloud SRE style DevOps. At the end of this chapter, you will understand

- How Monitoring works and learns logging activities on Google Cloud
- Why alerting is critical to SRE
- How to get the most out of our application using Google Cloud Services

Understanding Operations in Context

Operations, monitor, debug and enhance the application performance on your Google Cloud Environment. The verbs monitor, debug and enhance the scope of operations.

Key Operations

In the first step, we pull in the data gather logs, metrics, and traces from across the system. We visualize it with dashboards for built-in and customizable visualizations in the next step. We analyze and query those metrics, and in doing that, we establish performance and reliability indicators that are necessary for the SRE aspect of information. Operations integrate alerts triggered by user-definable criteria and error reporting.

Logging Management

Be it audit logs, user logs, or platform logs, it is the responsibility of the operations to deal with them. Logs can be exported for further analysis or just retained for a longer period. You can also discard to prevent them from burying by the volume of logs, or you can take them in and use them. This aspect of operations deals with error reporting, where the intent is to bring your app errors

clearly into focus. The interface also includes robust sorting and filtering capabilities, involving a lot of details, including occurrences, affected user count, first and last seen date, and cleaned exception stack trace. There is a list of previously known services as Stackdriver and are now under Google Cloud Operations Umbrella.

SRE Engagement Over Service Lifecycle

SRE refers to what happens when a software engineer is charged with what was formerly known as operations. We know that the goal of SLI is to measure how well a service is doing when the service is operational. SLIs are metrics over time, and the term metrics are used repetitively when monitoring operations. Part of the operations teams' job is to constantly monitor the reliability of their services to see if they are meeting their SLOs.

Site Reliability Engineers can be highly involved with the early development stages of an application during the limited availability phase. This time gives SRE a great opportunity to begin to measure and track their SLIs, review reliability, and set up their SLOs, which will eventually lead to the SLA specifics. Moreover, they can build their capacity models and establish incident responses which they will share with the development team. After a limited availability period, there is a general availability period. This is the period covered by operations.

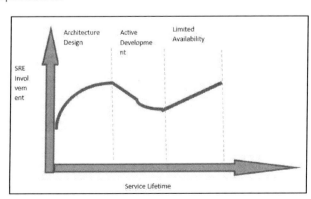

Ops Tools

We have Cloud Monitoring critical for tracking metrics, providing visualizing on a dashboard, and sending alerts

for all your cloud-based apps. Next, we have Cloud Logging, which offers granular details in a text-based, append-only format on every operation of every service on GCP. These two tools help SREs to evaluate SLIs and keep on track with their SLOs. Cloud Debugger is an essential service when a system encounters inevitable issues in real-time without impeding the app's execution or output. Cloud Trace maps out how exactly your service is processing various requests and responses it receives while tracking latency details and presenting them for analysis. Cloud Profiler keeps an eye on your code's performance, looking for bottlenecks as the code executes in production to increase efficiency and reduce costs.

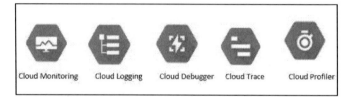

Monitoring Operations

Does Cloud monitoring tell how well your resources are performing? Are my applications meeting their SLOs and SLAs? Is anything wrong that requires immediate action or something that seems like it is wrong? Cloud monitoring is a complex system with many moving parts. There are three primary elements with their subcomponents which are our focus for now. First is the Workspace, which single pane of glass for viewing and monitoring data across projects. These projects can be on GCP or on AWS. Next is installed agents. This is an optional feature that will bring you additional application-specific metrics. It is not optional in certain situations if you want to get that data. Finally, we have alerts, which will notify you when something needs to be fixed.

Monitoring Workspaces

Workspace is Google Cloud's organizational tool for monitoring all your GCP and AWS resources. All your monitoring tools are contained in Workspace, including dashboards, alerts, charts, and more. A Workspace can host one or more projects, but a project has only one Workspace. Within the Workspace, information is viewed using Metrics, displayed in Charts, and grouped in Dashboards.

Monitoring Workspaces IAM Roles

Access to Workspaces and Cloud Monitoring are controlled by Cloud IAM. So, you can protect and manage who can view or edit your project's monitoring data. There are three key user roles: monitoring.viewer, monitoring.editor, and monitoring.admin. The viewer has just read-only access to view the metrics; an editor can edit workspaces and has to write access to the API and monitor console. Admin can do anything the editor can do, creating and assigning IAM roles. The monitoring.metric writer is a special role for service accounts permitting to write data to Workspaces by your application, but it does not provide read access.

Metrics

Metrics are raw data that GCP uses to create charts, and there are over 1500 pre-created metrics. These include the number of API calls, disk usage statistics, storage consumption, and more. You can create your custom metrics by addressing a built-in monitoring API, or you can use an open-source library such as **OpenCensus** to create those metrics. The best practice is not to create custom metrics.

There are four different metric data types: bool, a standard number, an int64, a double-precision, or string. These data types can be expressed in 2 different metric kinds. It can be a Gauge that measures the specific instant in time or a Delta that measures the change since the previous recording. Metrics are tied to specific resources such as virtual machines.

Without Monitoring, we would not be able to keep our site or app running reliably.

Managing Operations

Cloud Monitoring collects metrics with no additional configuration needed. There may be situations where you do not need a monitoring agent, but granular metrics can be collected using an optional monitoring agent. A monitoring agent can be used to gather third-party app metrics like those available from NGINX and Apache.

Monitoring Agents

There are two monitoring agents, one for Monitoring and the other for Logging. The monitoring agent for Monitoring is called collected, while the one for Logging is called fluentd. Both agents can be installed on Google

Compute VM Instances as well as on AWS EC2 instances. However, they are not supported on any other compute services because managed services either already have an agent installed or they do not require one.

External Integration Use Cases

We may need to work with third-party analytics tools such as Grafana. To do so, you need to pull metrics from the Monitoring API. Below is the metric of CPU Utilization on a Compute Engine Instance. It is presented in a ratio unit of type gauge with a double value type. The other reason you need to pull metrics through API is that you might want to store them for long-term analysis. Cloud Monitoring holds metrics for six weeks.

GKE Integration with Cloud Monitoring

Kubernetes engine is natively integrated with both Cloud Monitoring and Logging. An option titled Enable Cloud Operations for GKE is found in the cluster settings checked by default. Cloud Operations for GKE replaces Legacy Monitoring and Logging. GKE monitoring also works with third-party monitoring tools like Prometheus. The Kubernetes master component, Kubernetes cluster, Kubernetes node, Kubernetes pods, and Kubernetes container are the Kubernetes metrics that monitoring output collects.

Establishing Alerts

We need alerts because sometimes things break, and nobody wants to spend their time staring at a dashboard, and that is why we generate alerting policy. An alerting policy is made up of 3 main things. One or more conditions, such as a metric threshold that are either exceeded or not met. The conditions trigger an incident when thresholds are crossed in some way. The incident will include a notification with the name of the person to contact and how to contact him or her. Alert could contain not only bare details but some additional documentation with information on how to address an issue.

Establishing Alerts: IAM Roles

You can use Cloud Monitoring roles to create and edit alerting policies. There are three key user roles: monitoring.viewer, monitoring.editor, and monitoring.admin. Monitoring alert policy editor or viewer have minimal permission to create an alert via monitoring API.

Leveraging Logging Activities

Cloud logging is a Google Cloud service that is used for storing, viewing, and interacting with logs. Interaction here means reading and writing various logs entries, querying logs, exporting to other services – on and off a platform, creating metrics from logs so you can visualize what all that text is about. It also means interacting with aspects of Cloud Logging like Logs Viewer and API. There are multiple types of logs available. Logs are also used by other Cloud operation services such as debug and error reporting.

Logging IAM Roles

There are two different types of roles available for Cloud IAM in terms of Cloud Logging. There are generic roles that work with both users and service accounts and roles just for service accounts.

Service account roles include:

- *Logging Writer*: This allows you to write logs but does not allow you to view any other logs
- *Logging Bucket Writer*: This allows you to write logs to a specific bucket

The generic roles include:

- *Logging Viewer:* This can view any log except Data access and Access Transparency logs.
- *Logging Private Viewer:* This allows you to view everything
- *Logging Configuration Writer:* This allows you to create logs-based metrics, the buckets, the views, and export sinks
- *Logging Admin:* Gives you full access to all logging activities

Logs Types and Mechanics

The primary category includes security logs, Audit logs and Access Transparency logs, and non-security logs used to debug, troubleshoot, and monitor. The logs include User logs, Platform logs, VPC Flow Logs, and Firewall logs. Some logs are always enabled. These logs are not charged and have a retention period of 400 days. Others are manually enabled logs; they are charged according to the log information ingested with 30-day default retention, which is configurable.

Security Logs

Audit Logs

Google Cloud services keep track of administrative operations and access to your Google Cloud resources via audit logs. With the same level of transparency as on-premises systems, audit logs help you answer "who did what, where, and when?" within your Google Cloud resources. Enabling audit logs allows your security, auditing, and compliance teams to keep an eye on Google Cloud data and systems for any vulnerabilities or data misuse from outside sources.

Admin Activity Audit Logs

It keeps track of API calls and other operations that change resource configuration or metadata. These logs, for example, track when users create virtual machine instances or alter Identity and Access Management permissions.

You cannot configure, exclude, or disable Admin Activity audit logs because they are always written. Admin Activity audit logs are created even if the Cloud Logging API is disabled.

Data Access Audit Logs

API calls that read resource configuration or information and user-driven API calls that generate, edit, or read user-provided resource data are all included in the Data Access audit logs.

Audit logs are not generated for publicly accessible sites with the Identity and Access Management rules allAuthenticatedUsers or allUsers. Audit logs are not generated for resources that may be accessed without logging into a Google Cloud, Google Workspace, Cloud Identity, or Drive Enterprise account. This aids in the protection of end-user identities and data.

Data Access audit logs are disabled by default, with the exception of BigQuery Data Access audit logs, because audit logs can be extremely extensive. You must explicitly allow Data Access audit logs for Google Cloud services other than BigQuery if you want them to be written. If you enable the logs, your Cloud project may be charged for the consumption of the additional logs.

System Event Audit Logs

Log entries for Google Cloud activities that change resource settings can be found in the System Event audit logs. Google systems generate System Event audit logs; they are not triggered by direct user input.

You cannot configure, exclude, or disable System Event audit logs because they are constantly written.

Policy Denied Audit Logs

When a Google Cloud service restricts access to a user or service account due to a security policy violation, policy denied audit logs are created. VPC Service Controls determines the security policies and sends the Policy Denied audit records to Cloud Logging.

Policy Denied audit logs are generated by default, and the storage of the logs is charged to your Cloud project. Policy Denied audit logs cannot be disabled; however, you can use exclusion filters to prevent them from being absorbed and stored in Cloud Logging.

Access Transparency Logs

Google's long-term commitment to transparency and user trust includes Access Transparency. Google employees' acts when viewing customer content are recorded in the Access Transparency logs.

Cloud Audit Logs and Access Transparency Logs provide different information. Cloud Audit Logs document the actions conducted in your Google Cloud resources by members of your Google Cloud organization, whereas Access Transparency Logs document the actions taken by Google employees.

The affected resource and action, the time of the action, the rationale for the action, and information about the accessor are all included in the Access Transparency log entries.

Non-Security Logs

- **User Logs:** Generated by the software or applications, and they require a logging agent
- **Platform Logs:** Generated by the service themselves, such as compute engine startup script
- **VPC Flow Logs:** Look at the sample of network flow information sent or received by your virtual private cloud resources

- **Firewall Logs:** Captures effects of any allowing or denying of access

Logging Agent

The logging agents' purpose is to capture additional VM Logs. It includes any operating system logs or events. Third-party logs can also be generated by the logging agent. Logging agent is based on open-source data collector fluentd and is only applicable to Google Compute Engine and AWS EC2.

Optimize Performance With Trace and Profiler

Cloud Trace is a conveying that gathers idleness information from your applications and showcases it in the Google Cloud Console. Latency data is extremely important to any deployed application. Latency is a delay between when a request is issued, and a response is delivered. In SRE, you want your users to be satisfied and usability to be high.

Cloud Trace Primary Features

Cloud Trace is compatible with almost all Google Cloud assets, application motor VMS, and holders. It can also display aggregated latency metrics in general. It can also show general aggregated latency data. It can show any degradations that happen over time, and it is useful for identifying bottlenecks. It automatically alerts you if there is a big shift. Cloud Trace supports Java, Node.js, Ruby, and Go, and API is available to work with any source.

Cloud Profiler

Cloud Profiler constantly examines the presentation of CPU or memory-serious capacities executed across an application. So, Cloud Profiler is more of an operations concern than an SRE. Cloud Profiler helps you identify any functions of your code that are not optimal.

Cloud Profiler Primary Features

Cloud Profilers' primary target is to improve performance, and when your performance is improved, your cost is reduced. It supports Java, Python, Node.js, and Go. Cloud Profiler is agent-based which means you need to integrate code into your application to call the Cloud Profiler service. The code itself has an extremely low impact. The profile generated by Cloud Profiler can

be saved for 30 days. You can export the files for longer storage. Cloud Profiler is free.

Instrumenting Your Code for Cloud Trace

Google's client libraries are in four languages: Ruby, Node.js, C# ASP.NET Core, C# ASP.NET. There is also an open-source effort called OpenTelemetry that supports two languages: Node.js and Go. An older series of open-source libraries called OpenCensus support a different set of four languages: Python, Java, Go, and PHP.

Printed in Great Britain
by Amazon